BRYAN LEE O'MALLEY'S

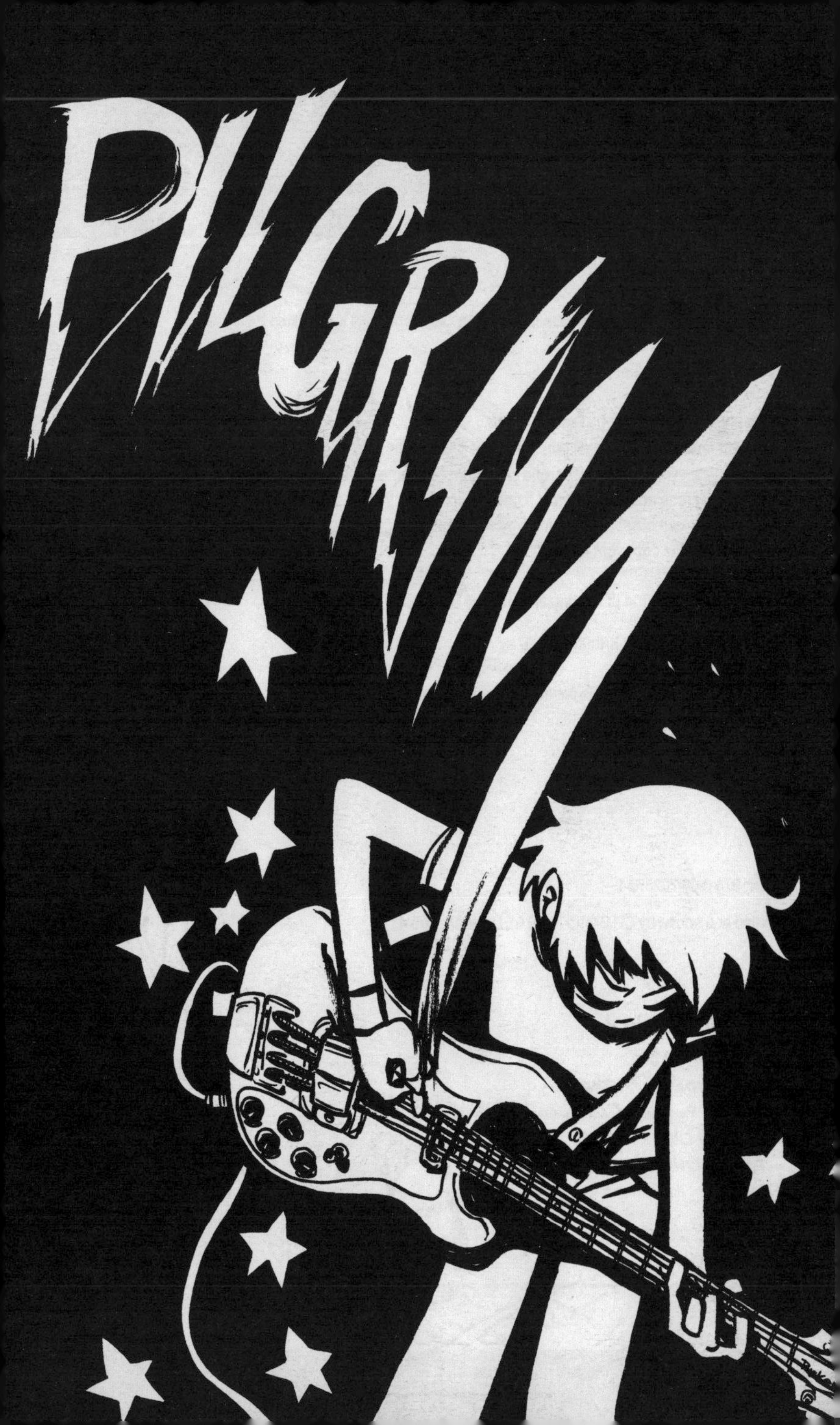
PILGRIM

edited by James Lucas Jones | design by Bryan Lee O'Malley & Keith Wood

Published by Fourth Estate

First published in 2004 in the United States by Oni Press.

First published in Great Britain in 2010 by
Fourth Estate
An imprint of HarperCollins*Publishers*
1 London Bridge Strret
London SE1 9GF
www.4thestate.co.uk

7

ISBN: 978-0-00-793079-1

Printed and bound by CP| Group (UK) Ltd, Croydon, CR0 4YY

special thanks to
  Hope Larson
  Christopher Butcher
  Carla, Amanda, Catriona & Lynette
  James Lucas Jones
  AND YOU.

DATING A HIGH SCHOOLER

JUST SO I TELL YOU BEFORE YOU HEAR SOME DIRTY LIES FROM SOMEONE ELSE, YES, I'M DATING A 17-YEAR-OLD.

WALLACE WELLS
ROOMMATE
25 YEARS OLD
RATING: 7.5/10

IS HE CUTE?

HA, HA, HA, HA, HA.

I / can't be sure / but I think I heard you / crawl thru the door / you / didn't say a word / and i think you tried to go to bed but instead you went to floor / you've been out drinking with the other boys again / telling them no we are only friends

Hey Kids! Now you can play along with Sex Bob-omb at home! It's easy, because they're kind of crappy! Look, this whole song only uses 3 chords!

4/4 rock, fast, hard, sloppy

end / and where do you begin? / you've been out partying with guys i've never met / drinking beer and smoking cigarettes killing brain cells and killing me / oh stop pretending / that this isn't really ending / and I will stop resenting you

RIIIIING

RIIIING

SCOTT W. PILGRIM
Wallace P. Weldon
JUNK MAIL PLZ.

RIIIIING

RIIIIINGy

...HELLO?

SCOTT? DID I WAKE YOU UP? IT'S TWELVE THIRTY!!!!

STACEY PILGRIM
19 YEARS OLD
YOUNGER SISTER
RATING: "T" FOR TEEN

OHH... NO... I'VE TOTALLY BEEN AWAKE FOR SEVERAL HOURS.

SEVERAL.

YEAH, RIGHT! WHAT'S THIS I HEAR ABOUT YOU DATING A SIXTEEN-YEAR OLD?!?!

WHO-EVER'S BAND IT IS, I REALLY LIKE IT.

WELL, THANKS.

I DON'T LISTEN TO THAT MUCH MUSIC, AND, I MEAN, I KNOW A LOT OF KIDS WHO PLAY PIANO OR WHATEVER, BUT YOU GUYS *ROCK*.

I KNEW THAT I PERSONALLY ROCKED, BUT I NEVER SUSPECTED THAT WE ROCKED AS A UNIT. THANK YOU, KNIVES.

HMM, THIS IS ACTUALLY PRETTY CUTE. TOO BAD IT'S WINTER...

HEY, SPRING'S AROUND THE CORNER. TRY IT ON.

NO, NO... I MEAN...

...I MEAN, IT'S NOT LIKE I'D BUY IT.

SIP

DUDE, I'M TOTALLY NOT DREAMING!

W-WHAT?

DUDE, SHE'S TOTALLY REAL!!

WHO?

SCOTT, I FORBID YOU FROM HITTING ON RAMONA, EVEN IF YOU *HAVEN'T* HAD A GIRLFRIEND IN OVER A YEAR.

DUDE, HE'S GOING OUT WITH A HIGH SCHOOLER RIGHT NOW. HIS MOURNING PERIOD IS OFFICIALLY OVER.

UGH... SCOTT, SHE'S TOO GOOD FOR YOU, OKAY? LET'S LEAVE IT AT THAT.

AND ANYWAY, I'M NOT EVEN SURE IF SHE REALLY DID HAVE A BIG BREAKUP.

SHE'S KIND OF VAGUE ABOUT IT, SO I HAD TO PIECE IT TOGETHER INTUITIVELY. SHE JUST KEEPS MENTIONING SOME GUY NAMED GIDEON...

I DON'T KNOW WHAT IT IS ABOUT THAT GIRL. SHE JUST--

FORGET ABOUT IT, SCOTT!

4

RAMONA COME CLOSER

NICE ONE, SCOTT!
NOW TURN THE PAGE.

24 HRS

LATER

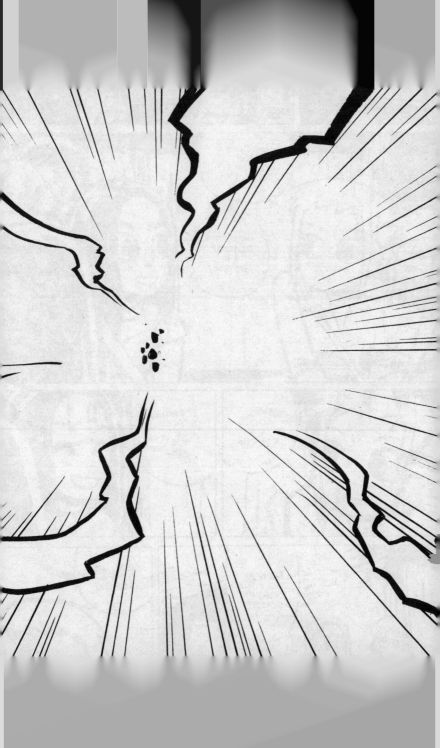

GIRLZ

UM... ARE YOU RELATED TO SCOTT?

SCOTT PILGRIM? I'M HIS SISTER!

OH, COOL... I'M RAMONA.

I'M STACEY. NICE TO MEET YOU!

SO HOW DO YOU KNOW SCOTT?

HE'S... UM, HE'S A FRIEND.

UPSET PEOPLE ROCK

MATTHEW PATEL WAS THE ONLY NON-WHITE, NON-JOCK KID IN SCHOOL. PROBABLY THE ONLY ONE FOR MILES AROUND, OR IN THE ENTIRE STATE, FOR ALL I KNOW. SO, OF COURSE...

KISSY KISSY

E JOINED FORCES AND TOOK 'EM ALL OUT. WE WERE ONE HELL OF A TEAM. NOTHING OULD BEAT MATTHEW'S MYSTICAL POWERS COMBINED WITH MY BRUTE STRENGTH.

NOTHING BUT PRE-ADOLESCENT CAPRICIOUSNESS.

TO BE
CONTINUED

NEXT!

Does Scott & Ramona's burgeoning relationship have a future? Isn't Scott still supposedly dating Knives Chau? Who is Ramona's second evil ex-boyfriend, and why is he in Toronto? Who are The Clash At Demonhead, and what kind of bizarre art-punky music do they play? Who's their hot girl keyboardist, and what's her relation to Scott? Why are they Knives Chau's new favorite band? Fights! Drama! Secrets revealed! The answers to all these questions and more! It's all coming in...

SCOTT PILGRIM
VERSUS THE WORLD

BRYAN LEE O'MALLEY

LOVED BY ANIMALS

Illustration of the Author by Corey S. Lewis The Rey

BRYAN LEE O'MALLEY has been alive since 1979. He plays some guitar and keyboards, but is pretty bad at bass. His first book was called **LOST AT SEA**. His second book is this one. You can learn more about him at **WWW.RADIOMARU.COM**